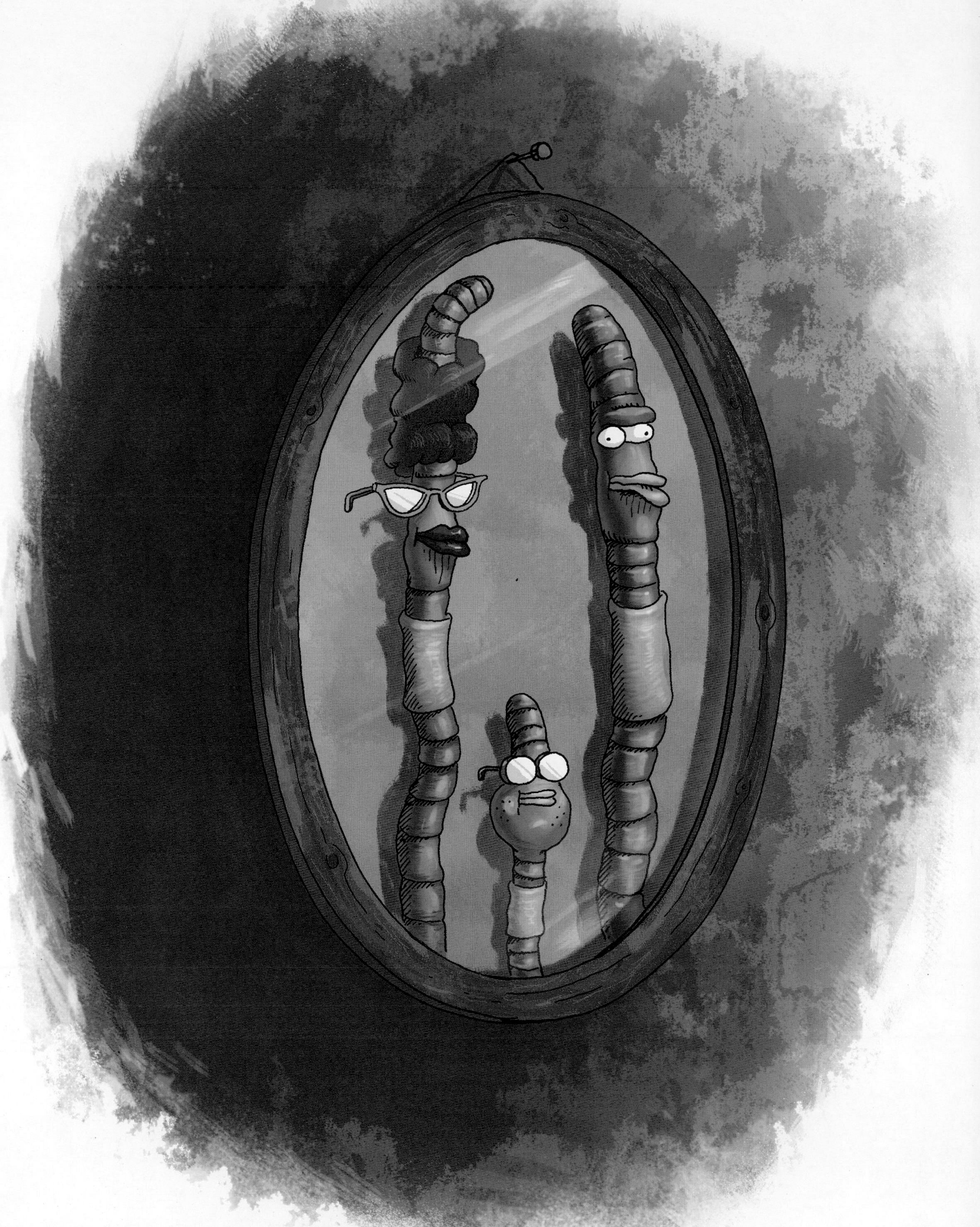

There's A HAIR In My Dirt!

A WORM'S STORY

Gary Larson

Foreword by Edward O. Wilson

LITTLE, BROWN AND COMPANY

For Toni,
Who always believed

A Little, Brown Book
First published in Great Britain in 1998
THERE'S A HAIR IN MY DIRT! A WORM'S STORY. Copyright © 1998 by FarWorks, Inc.
Art coloured by Nick Bell of Wildstorm Productions
First published in the United States of America by HarperCollins Publishers, Inc.
The moral right of the author has been asserted.

A CIP catalogue record for the book is available in the British Library.

ISBN 0–316–64519–2

Printed and bound in Great Britain by Butler & Tanner Ltd, Frome and London

Little, Brown and Company (UK)
Brettenham House
Lancaster Place
London WC2E 7EN

Foreword
by Edward O. Wilson

Attention, fellow Larsonites! This is a serious book. It's about an earthworm family, a comely maiden, and what really goes on in the natural world. What better author than America's Aesop to tell us the truth about the little creatures that run the earth? Who better qualified to explain ecology than the madcap sage of the biological sciences whose extravagantly admired cartoons already festoon laboratory bulletin boards across the land? And what better way to present the subject than by elevating the creatures to our line of sight, not by lofting them to eye level but by bringing our chins to the ground?

Like all great humorists, Gary Larson has a moral embedded in his story. Actually, it's stronger than that. The saga of the maiden is embedded in the moral, which is reinforced with a redemptive laugh on every page. The moral is this: Nature is part of us and we are part of Nature. Larson describes what we biologists have known all along, that Nature really *is* red in tooth and claw. While it is true that all organisms are dependent on others, the ecological web they create is built entirely from mutual exploitation. Life is tough! There is no free lunch, and what one creature consumes, another must provide. I know of no instance in which a species of plant or animal gives willing support to another without extracting some advantage in return. The fields and woodland across which trips our lovely damsel are bought with a price, paid mostly by the naive and unsuspecting.

Homo sapiens is no exception to this iron rule of Nature. So Professor Larson delivers Ecology 101—worth two college credits—and with hilarity, which everyone needs when adjusting to reality. Humor can be defined as surprise that softens our perception of adversity to a psychologically manageable level. It is a deep and primitive response. The human laugh, some biologists believe, evolved from an explosive expiration still preserved in the chimpanzee's "Ah!," which is part of the ape's relaxed open-mouth display. To get the primordial feel, try it the chimp way yourself: Grin, open your mouth slightly, and exhale repetitively, Ah! Ah! Ah! Relaxing, right?

The point is that we, too, are organisms. We are subject to the same physical laws, still tied to the planet, totally enmeshed in food webs, energy flows, nutrient cycles, predator-prey cycles, territorial imperatives, and even slavery of other species, such as cows and dogs. Nature is to be loved, cherished, admired, and yes, poetically celebrated (Why not? We've depended on it for millions of years), but, above all, understood. The maiden, as you will see as the narrative unfolds, might have enjoyed her saunter better if she had understood.

So let the worm family go back to eating dirt with pride. We all need one another, each in our special niche. As for us—well, when you have finished reading this remarkable book, just watch where you step; be careful of little lives.

Beneath the floor of a very old forest, nestled in among some nice, rich topsoil, lived a family of worms. Earthworms, to be exact.

One evening, the three of them—father, mother, and their little worm son—sat down to their usual dinner: dirt.

They had just begun to dine when the little worm,
staring wide-eyed at his meal, suddenly spit out his
food and screamed, "THERE'S A HAIR IN MY DIRT!
THERE'S A HAIR IN MY DIRT!"

And sure enough, there it was—plain as day. They could all see it.

At first, the little worm was horrified, but soon that gave way to being just plain mad.

"I hate being a worm!" he screeched, his tiny body trembling. "We're the lowest of the low! Bottom of the food chain! Bird food! Fish bait! What kind of life is this, anyway? We never go swimming or camping or hiking or *anything!* Shoot, we never even go to the surface unless the rains flood us out! All we ever do is crawl around in the stupid ground. Oh, and how can I forget? We eat dirt! Dirt for breakfast, dirt for lunch, and dirt for dinner! Dirt, dirt, dirt! And look—now there's even a hair in my dirt! The final insult— I can't stand it any longer! I HATE BEING A WORM!"

And with that, the little worm slumped back in his chair, exhausted by his outburst.

Mother Worm, an expression of concern on her face, looked from her pouting son to Father Worm. She had constantly tried to make their home as cheery as possible, even going so far as always putting silverware on the table—despite the fact that none of them had arms.

But Father Worm, a proud invertebrate and a learned member of the Annelida phylum (even with his small, rudimentary brain), was glaring at what he considered to be an ungrateful and ignorant son. "Well, well, well," he said, breaking the awkward silence. "Let me get this straight: Not only is your mother's dirt not good enough for you, but you feel being a worm isn't exactly a charmed life, eh?" A strange glint fell across Father Worm's eye. "My boy, I think it's time I tell you a story."

The little worm looked up and sneered sarcastically, "If this is the one about the teenager worms and the Insane Trout Fisherman, I've heard that one a gazillion times!"

"No, no," Father Worm calmly responded. "Not that story. (Though it is a good story.) This one is different. *This* story has a happy ending."

"I have an idea!" Mother Worm chimed in enthusiastically. "Let's listen to Father's story and afterwards, maybe we can all have some fresh, cold dirt for dessert!"

I'm in hell.

And so Father Worm cleared his long, primitive pharynx, took a futile puff on his dirt-filled pipe, and began his story.

Once upon a time, in a forest not too far from here, lived a beautiful young maiden. Her name was Harriet, and Harriet loved the magic of Nature, with all its magnificent plants and animals.

One lovely spring morning, she decided to take a stroll along her favorite woodland trail. "What wondrous things will I see today?" Harriet thought to herself. I must say, she was as excited as a tapeworm in a meat patty!

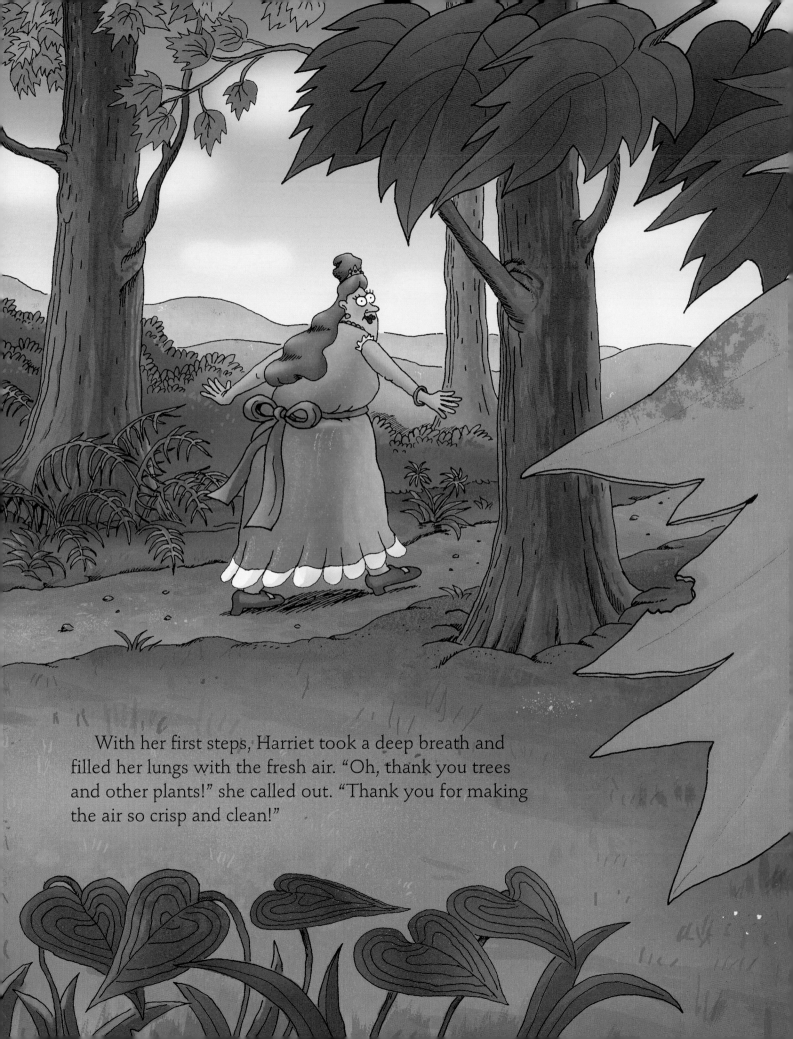

With her first steps, Harriet took a deep breath and filled her lungs with the fresh air. "Oh, thank you trees and other plants!" she called out. "Thank you for making the air so crisp and clean!"

Well, as any worm with a half a ganglion knows, the plants did a little more than just make the air crisp and clean—they made the air *air*! Every molecule of oxygen in the earth's atmosphere was put there by a plant, and—last time I looked—the Living were quite fond of oxygen. (Heck, even the Dead need it, or they'd hang around a lot longer and get on everyone's nerves.)

FIELD GUIDE TO THE HUMANS

LOGGER
Makes loud noise. Usually found near areas with lots of stumps.

HUNTER
Dangerous. Watch out for exploding stick. Without stick, quite defenseless.

MUSHROOMER
Usually seen in spring and summer. Shy, secretive, always looking down. Good eating.

ELVIS
Strictly nocturnal. Sometimes fat, sometimes thin. Very rare if not, in fact, dead.

BEAUTIFUL MAIDEN
Cottage dweller. Usually seen with stupid grin on face. Loves plants, animals, and chiffon dresses. Diurnal.

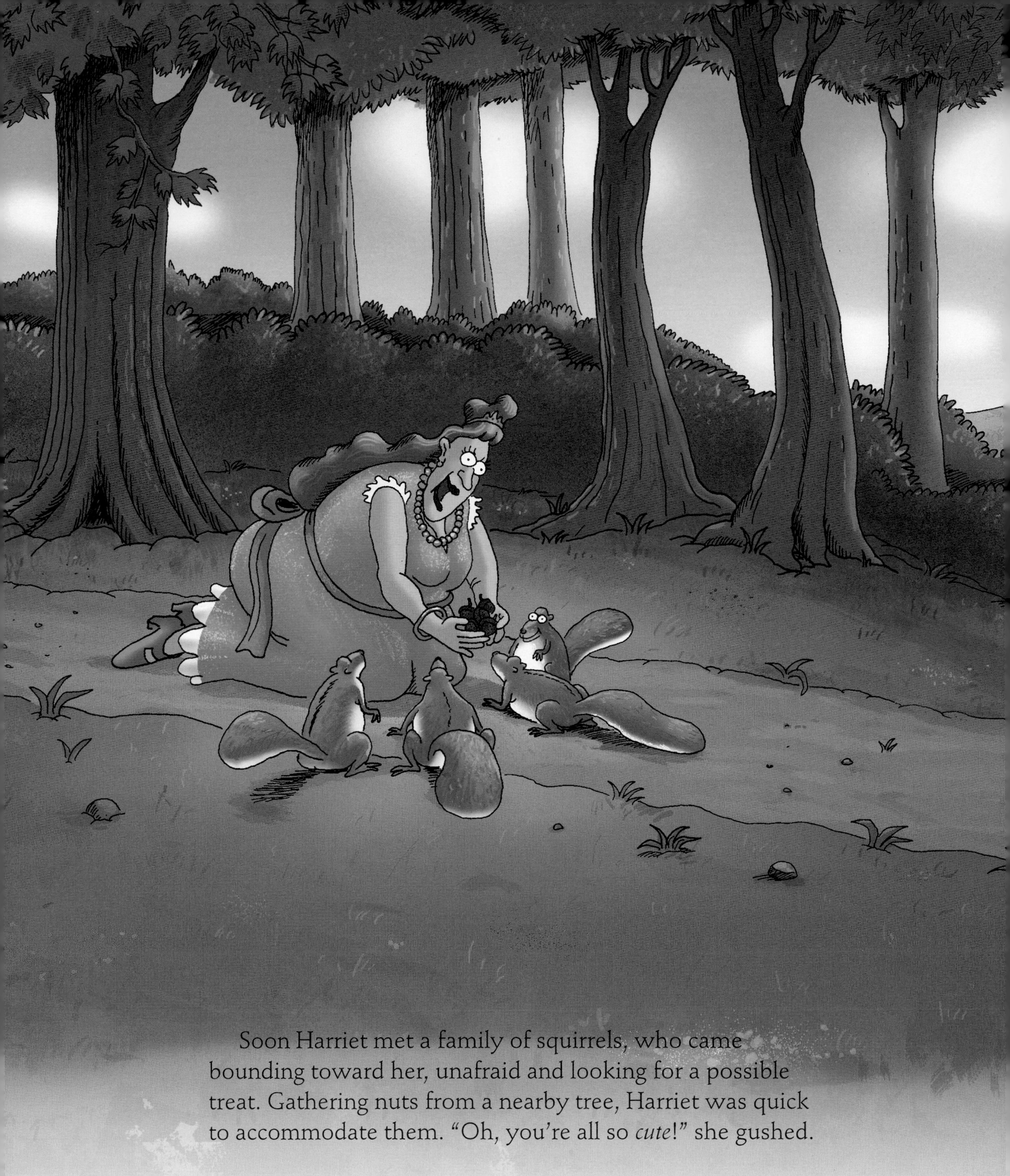

Soon Harriet met a family of squirrels, who came bounding toward her, unafraid and looking for a possible treat. Gathering nuts from a nearby tree, Harriet was quick to accommodate them. "Oh, you're all so *cute*!" she gushed.

To be sure, these furry creatures had that "cute" thing down real good—regrettably. You see, Harriet was feeding Gray squirrels, a large, aggressive species that had been introduced to this forest and were taking it over from the native Red squirrels, a smaller, more timid species.

All squirrels are rodents, but in the wrong time and place, some are rats.

Around the bend, the forest opened into a meadow of wild flowers as far as the eye could see. "My!" Harriet exclaimed, bedazzled. "I'm gazing at a painting! Oh, Mother Nature! What an artist you are!"

"Oh, Mother Nature! What a sex maniac you are!" may have been a better choice of words, for Harriet was actually gazing upon a reproductive battlefield. Using bright colors, nectar, mimicry, deception, and whatever other tricks they had up their leaves, these floral sirens were competing for the attention of pollinating insects.

In a field of flowers, all is fair in bugs and war.

A little ways farther, Harriet happened to look down and saw a column of ants crossing the trail. "Ahh!" She smiled, noticing all the eggs they were carrying. "Even the littlest creatures take good care of their babies! How adorable!"

"Adorable?" Well, as Grandpa Worm used to say, "About as adorable as a nest of baby robins!" These were Amazon ants, a species that, despite its name, lives in many parts of the world and specializes in the enslavement of other species—and Harriet was watching a raiding party returning home with their living booty.

Is that you, Mom?

Author's Note: Although most slave ants spend their lives toiling away (e.g., getting up early to milk the aphids), a few escape that fate by doting on the queen. Entomologists often describe these slackers as "abdomen kissers."

As the trail widened and the trees thinned out, Harriet heard a rumbling sound. Looking up, she spied a familiar truck heading her way. She immediately recognized the ruggedly handsome and rosy-cheeked character behind the wheel. "Hello, Lumberjack Bob!" she called, waving with happy excitement, knowing him to be a gentle man with a quick smile and a big heart.

Well, kind, big-hearted, and rosy-cheeked he might be (the latter caused by expanded capillaries in his skin's dermal layer), but Lumberjack Bob was really just a regular guy with little education doing the one job he knew how to do—cutting down ancient trees that were here long before the first intestinal worms came over in the Pilgrims.

Harriet then heard a magical sound from the canopy of trees above. "Oh!" she cried skyward. "Listen to the songs of those happy, happy birds!"

Well, if those birds were happy, may the garden gods cut me in half with a rusty shovel! Birds sing to communicate, and what they were communicating was mostly an array of insults, warnings, and come-ons to members of their own species.

(In fact, all baby birds are taught by their parents not to even smile, or their beaks will crack.)

This *story* is for the birds, if you ask me!" the little worm interrupted suddenly. "Some lady taking a walk in the woods? Oh, I can't *stand* the excitement!

"If you have to tell me a story, you could at least tell me one that's sort of exciting—like 'Mr. Dung Beetle Finds His Field of Dreams.' Now that's a cool story!"

"I'm telling you *this* story," said Father Worm, rather testily. "So just put a fish hook in that mouth of yours and let me finish! Now where was I? Oh, yes."

In the distance, Harriet noticed some movement at the far side of the meadow. "Fawns!" she happily exclaimed. And as she watched them taking turns chasing each other and frolicking while their mother grazed, she mused out loud, "Yes, little ones, go ahead and play your silly games, for soon you'll be all grown-up and have to say good-bye to such carefree antics."

Silly games? Carefree antics? Leech livers! As young animals play, they literally become smarter, as extra neurons are formed in their brains. And, of course, smarter deer have a better chance of survival than dumber ones.

You know, Bambi's mom never played much as a kid, and look what happened to *her*.

Around the next bend, the path skirted a lovely pond, and Harriet was elated to see a slow-moving, lumpy creature just in front of her.

"Mr. Turtle!" she squealed, excitedly scooping up the startled reptile. And then, with a sympathetic smile, she added, "What are you doing out of your pond, Mr. Turtle? Well, I think I'll just send you right back home!"

So Harriet wound up and hurled the bewildered animal into the middle of the marsh, where it landed with a loud and satisfying *kerplunk!*

Well, unfortunately, "Mr. Turtle" was not a turtle at all, but a tortoise, and while turtles are well adapted for aquatic life, their land-dwelling cousins never even evolved into decent dogpaddlers. Sadly, the little reptile sank to the bottom, where it promptly drowned. (Even worse, who knows how many of our parasitic loved ones went down with the ship!)

As the middle of the pond bubbled, Harriet's eye was caught by large and colorful insects flying just above the surface. "Dragonflies!" she exulted. "Oh, look how they dance in the air, like winged ballerinas!"

"Winged ballerinas?" Winged assassins in tutus might have been closer to the truth! Dragonflies are skilled predators, and if their graceful aerobatics have anything to do with dancing, then I'm a sea monkey's uncle.

Harriet thought she saw something move in the tall grass near her feet. Dropping gracefully to her knees, she almost put her hand on a small slug that was wandering by. Recoiling in disgust, she cried, "Stay away from me, you slimy little thing!"

And then, seeing the real object of her desire, she lunged forward and came up with her prize. "Hello, Mr. Frog!" she said, laughing. "Should I kiss you and see if you turn into a prince?"

Fortunately for Harriet, she *didn't* kiss
this little creature, for it wasn't "Mr. Frog"
she was holding, but "Mr. Toad," and like
most toads (and some frogs), this one packed
a powerful, sometimes lethal, toxin in its skin.
On the other hand, the slug slime was actually
quite harmless, if perhaps a bit gooey.

Kissing out
of your species
is not really
recommended,
Son, but if you have to,
always choose a gastropod
over an amphibian.

"Ernie Johnson!" Mother Worm suddenly blurted out. "What?" Father Worm asked, finding his story interrupted for the second time. "Ernie Johnson!" his wife repeated. "I went to my high school prom with a slug named Ernie Johnson! And Ernie's slime might have been harmless, dear, but it certainly wrecked *my* evening! Before the night was over, I was wishing I had brought a salt shaker!"

"Well, what made you fall for Dad?" the little worm asked. "He's slimy, too, isn't he?"

"No, not exactly," Mother Worm replied. "Your father has always been more on what I'd call the 'sticky' side."

"MAY I PLEASE CONTINUE?" screamed Father Worm. "That is, if the two of you are through discussing the viscosity of my mucus!"

Releasing the frog, Harriet continued on her way. The trail soon brought her to the edge of a small river, where she saw a most remarkable sight: Large, hook-nosed fish, their red scales shimmering in the sunlight, were struggling to get upstream. "Salmon!" she joyfully declared. "Looking for their spawning grounds, I bet!"

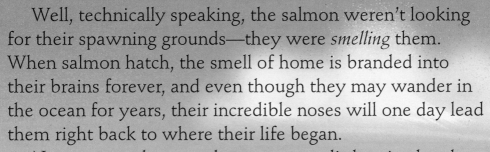

Well, technically speaking, the salmon weren't looking for their spawning grounds—they were *smelling* them. When salmon hatch, the smell of home is branded into their brains forever, and even though they may wander in the ocean for years, their incredible noses will one day lead them right back to where their life began.

Now, we earthworms have our own little miracle when it comes to breeding: Each of us contains *both* male and female reproductive organs! (But that's a story I'll tell you when you're a little longer, Son.)

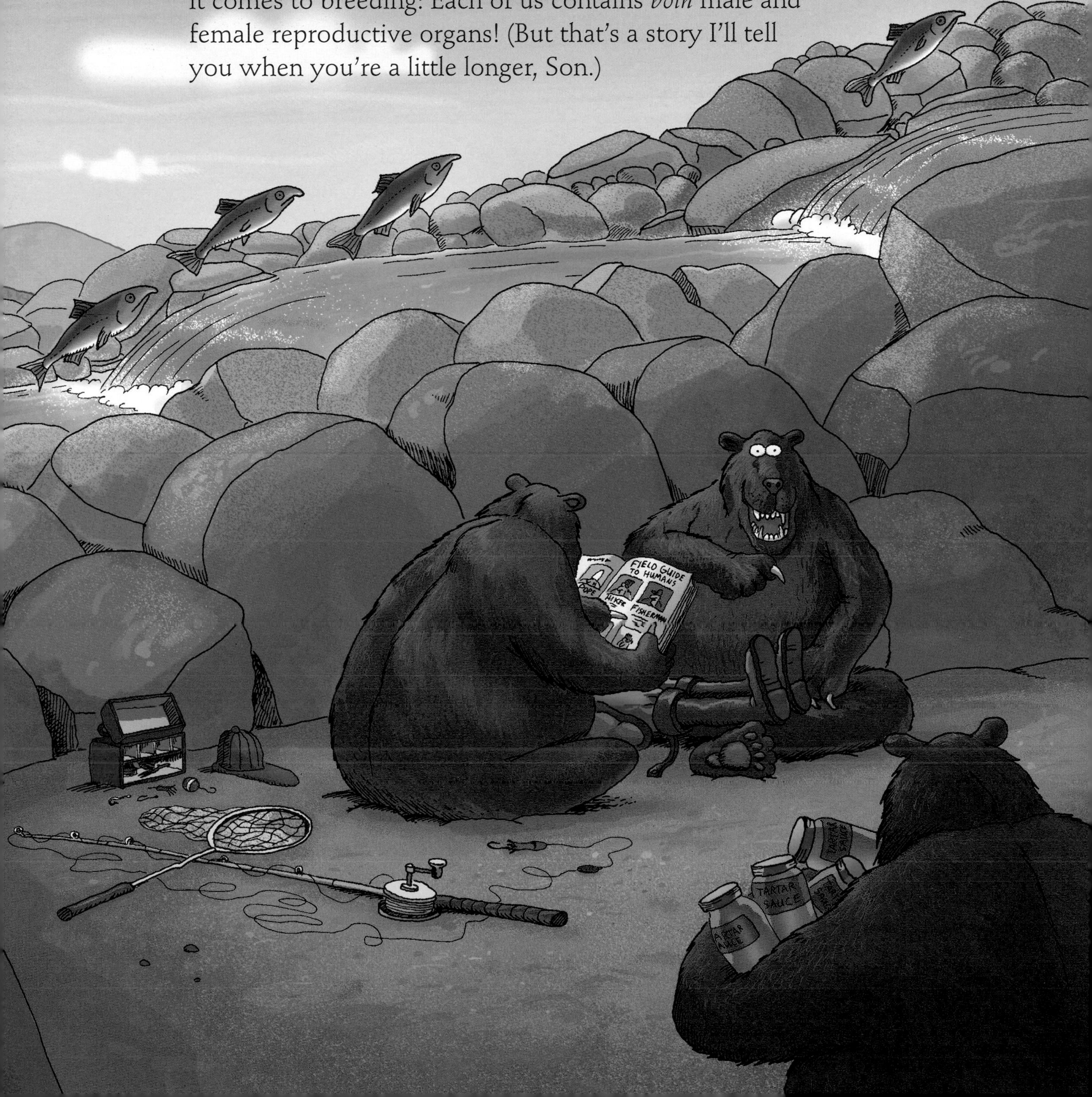

FIELD GUIDE TO HUMANS
POPE
HIKER
FISHERMAN
TARTAR SAUCE
TARTAR SAUCE

As the trees closed in on Harriet, the forest grew darker and darker. Sensing that she was being watched, Harriet looked up into a nearby tree and was momentarily startled to see a pair of large, ominous eyes staring back at her. "Oh, I recognize you now, Mr. Owl!" She laughed. "And fireflies!" she gleefully cried as a group of the little insects suddenly swarmed around her. "They're the fairies of the night, enchanting the forest with their magical little lights!"

Ha! Did Harriet ever get taken in by one of the oldest tricks in Nature's book—the old I'm-a-scary-creature-with-giant-eyeballs gag. You see, "Mr. Owl" was really a Royal moth, an insect that uses its large wingspots to mimic a much more frightening animal. (One once scared the dirt out of me!) And those fireflies—which really weren't fireflies at all, but beetles—were using a cold chemical process to produce light and attract potential mates. Beautiful, yes, but if anyone thinks they're magical, I've got some hardpan in Florida to sell them.

Soon our maiden was confronted by a sight that saddened her deeply. An immense tree, as old as the forest itself, was lying on the ground. "Oh, I'm so sorry!" Harriet said, touching the fallen giant. "Such a tragedy! Such a waste! Oh, you poor, beautiful tree!"

Well, truthfully, the tree's fate was a far cry from being a "waste." These huge "nurse trees," as their name implies, are the key to new growth and the survival of the entire forest. In fact, a fallen tree is arguably more alive than a standing one, so much of their mass is taken up with other organisms. As a famous worm once wrote,

> *I think that I shall never see*
> *a poem as lovely as*
> *a big, rotting tree carcass.*

Harriet was suddenly surprised to come across a little baby bird lying helplessly on the ground. She gently scooped up the scared little creature and searched for a nest in the highest reaches of a nearby tree. "Poor little guy," she cooed. "Did you fall out of your home? Well, I'll put you right back where you belong!"

Climbing the tree, Harriet peered into the nest. "There you go!" she said, placing the trembling baby bird alongside its sibling. "You two youngsters are together again!"

But not for long. As soon as Harriet was gone, the fledgling found itself plummeting back to earth. You see, she had rescued a baby Golden eagle, a species in which the strongest sibling ensures its own survival by giving its younger brothers and sisters the old "heave-ho."

Author's Note: This behavior always takes place in the parents' absence, which would come as no surprise to the younger siblings of all other species.

Scrambling up the tree, Harriet's view was marred by the sight of a forest fire, raging out of control, but fortunately moving away from her. "Oh, the suffering! The loss of life!" she lamented. "Someone should try and put it out!"

Someone should just mind their own business, from Nature's point of view.

Big, healthy trees don't burn very easily, unless the flames are stoked with a lot of fallen branches and debris. Occasional fires (if certain two-legged vertebrates would just let them run their course) benefit the forest by keeping all that dangerous "kindling" from piling up. But, boy, if it does pile up, *WHOOSH!*, better watch your anterior end.

But Harriet's spirits didn't stay dampened for long, and she decided it was time to return home. As she hummed a cheery tune, she reflected on how lucky she was to live in the forest and be so close to Nature. Oh, the things she had seen!

But then, without warning, Harriet came across something she didn't want to see. A sight that chilled her blood!

"A SNAKE!" she screamed. And trapped within the serpent's coils, being slowly suffocated, was a small, helpless mouse. The poor creature, almost expired, was emitting faint squeaks, and his scared eyes seemed to meet Harriet's in one last look of hope.

Acting quickly, Harriet grabbed
a nearby stick and began striking
the reptile repeatedly.
"Take that, you dreadful thing!"
BONK!
"And that!"
BONK!
"And two more!"
BONK! BONK!

Soon it was over. The snake was dead. (Boy, was he ever.)

Catching her breath, Harriet reached down and gently removed the unconscious mouse from the snake's lifeless coils. And as the fair maiden watched, a miracle occurred: The little mouse stirred. He was alive! A minute later, he got groggily to his feet, looked up at Harriet, and wiggled his nose.

Harriet beamed. As she held the little mouse in one hand, she wiped a tear away with the other.

She put the little fellow down at her feet, where he quickly bounded off into the tall grass, safe and sound. Harriet headed home. Good had triumphed over Evil, and the forest was just a little bit safer for everyone.

Well, actually, the snake Harriet killed was a Kingsnake, an efficient, rodent-eating predator, and that "cute" little mouse she saved was a vector for a deadly disease. When Harriet wiped the tear from her eye, a virus, which was living on the mouse's fur, invaded her body. And one lovely spring morning, Harriet, delirious with fever, stumbled out of her little cottage, fell over, and died.

The End.

"SHE DIED?" the little worm yelled. "What kind of story is that? That's supposed to cheer me up? Boy, I'm *really* full of warm, wormy feelings now! Thanks, Dad!"

Father Worm sat back in his chair, trying to be patient but secretly thinking his son was perhaps short a neuron or two. "Look, my boy," he said. "I'm afraid you haven't quite grasped the point of this story."

"You see," Father Worm began, "Harriet loved Nature. But loving Nature is not the same as understanding it. And Harriet not only misunderstood the things she saw—vilifying some creatures while romanticizing others—but also her own connection to them." Father Worm paused, his eyes narrowing. "Ah, connections, Son. That's the fateful key that Harriet missed, the key to understanding the natural world."

Father Worm sat back, stretching himself out to his full, glorious three and a half inches. "Take us worms, for example. We till, aerate, and enrich the earth's soil, making it suitable for plants. No worms, no plants; and no plants, no so-called higher animals running around with their oh-so-precious backbones!"

He was really getting into it now. "Heck, we're invertebrates, my boy! As a whole, we're the movers and shakers on this planet! Spineless superheroes, that's what *we* are!" And since Father Worm didn't have a fist to bring down on the table, he just yelled, "*BANG!*"

The little worm sat there for a moment, thinking about
what his father had just told him. And it was true, he was
feeling a little better about his lot in life. Maybe even a
little proud.

But then he remembered something.

"Okay, I get it—being a worm ain't so bad. But you're wrong about one thing: That story didn't have a happy ending! You said it had a *happy* ending!"

“Well, it does,” replied his father, “if you’re a worm.” And then he leaned across the table until his face was very, very close to his son’s and said, with a big grin, “Which brings us back to that hair in your dirt. Or should I say…

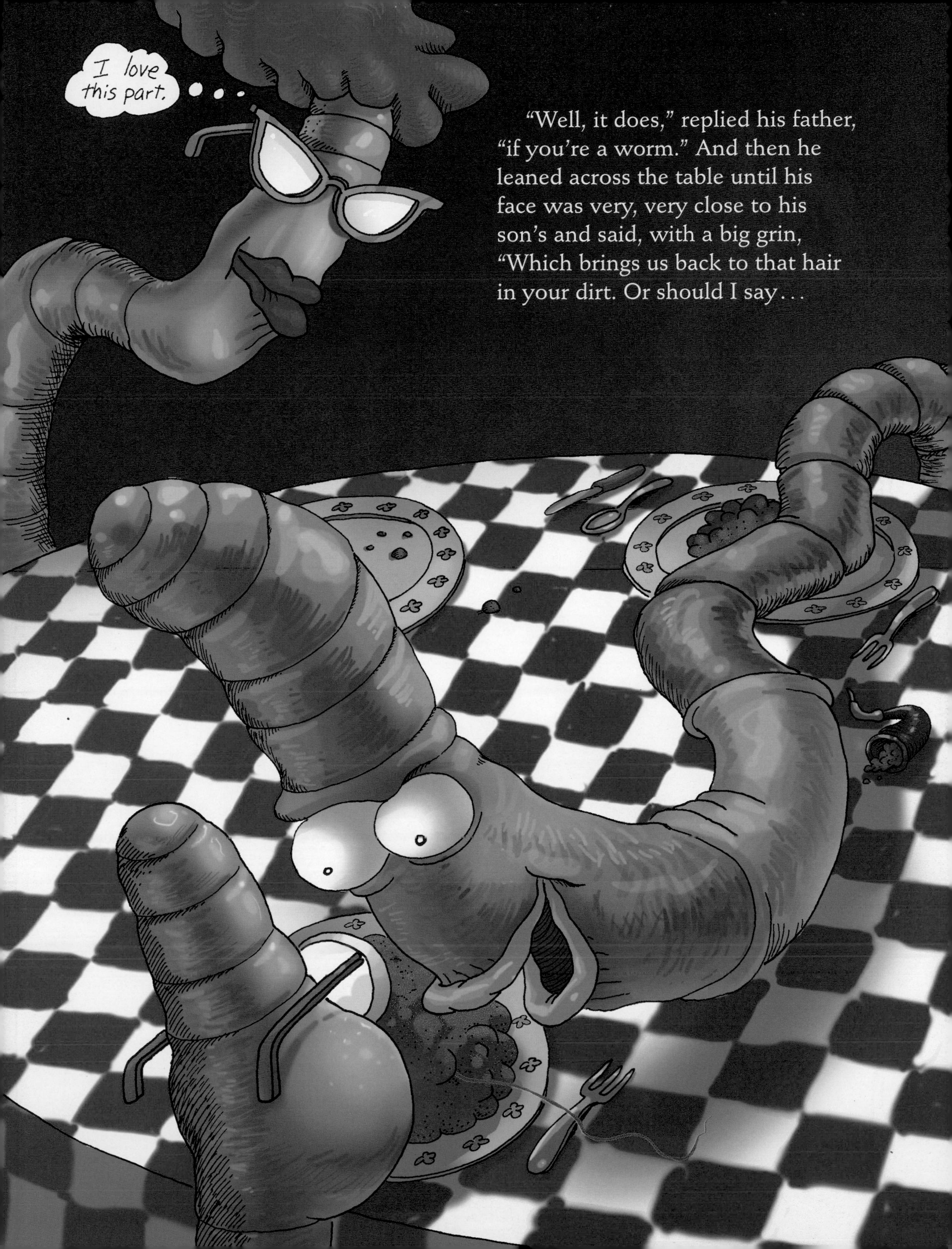
I love this part.

'. . . Harriet'?"

Mother giggled. Father guffawed. And the son
frowned, then smiled, then broke out in laughter.
   And after they all stopped laughing, the little worm
finished his whole dinner, went to bed, and had the best
dreams ever!

Author's Note: Well, truthfully, earthworms don't really sit around dinner tables complaining, telling stories, laughing, and so on. On the other hand, they do have a message for all of us,